THE GREAT PHILOSOPHERS

Consulting Editors
Ray Monk and Frederic Raphael

R. G. COLLINGWOOD

Aaron Ridley

ROUTLEDGE
New York

Published in 1999 by
Routledge
29 West 35th Street
New York, NY 10001

First published in 1997 by
Phoenix
A Division of the Orion Publishing Group Ltd.
Orion House
5 Upper Saint Martin's Lane
London WC2H 9EA

10 9 8 7 6 5 4 3 2 1

Library of Congress Cataloging-in-Publication Data

Ridley, Aaron.
    R. G. Collingwood / Aaron Ridley.
      p. cm.—(The great philosophers : 21)
    Includes bibliographical references.
    ISBN 0-415-92399-9 (pbk.)
    1. Collingwood, R. G. (Robin George), 1889–1943—
    Aesthetics. 2. Aesthetics. I. Title. II. Series: Great
    Philosophers (Routledge (Firm)) : 21.
B1618.C74R53 1999
111'.85'092—dc21
                                               99-14467
                                                     CIP

ACKNOWLEDGEMENTS

My thanks to Peter Johnson, Alex Neill and David Owen for their comments on earlier versions of this essay.

CONTENTS

R. G. COLLINGWOOD

A Philosophy of Art

INTRODUCTION

It is now clear that R.G. Collingwood (1889–1943) was one of the twentieth century's few outstanding philosophers of art. He wasn't only that. In books such as *Speculum Mentis*, *Essay on Metaphysics*, *The Idea of Nature*, *The New Leviathan*, *Essay on Philosophical Method* and, above all, *The Idea of History*, Collingwood made distinctive and sometimes important contributions to a number of areas of philosophy. But, for me at least, it is his philosophy of art that is really unignorable. From the early *Outlines of a Philosophy of Art*, through scattered essays, chapters and reviews to the final, mature position worked out in *The Principles of Art*, Collingwood's aesthetics stands out for its extraordinary combination of artistic, intellectual and ethical seriousness. Most recent aestheticians have not been particularly adept as critics or as artists; and so their engagement with the arts has tended to be driven more by their pre-existing philosophical concerns than by any special perplexities that the experience or the practice of art has raised in them. They have not, in that sense anyway, taken art seriously. Collingwood, by contrast, comes at art with the eye and the ear of a gifted draughtsman and amateur musician, and with an ability to write about the arts that most professional critics would envy, or should if they don't. He is also convinced that art matters. It does not embarrass him to think that art, apart from being a uniquely human activity, is a uniquely important one. In this he again distinguishes himself from the run of Anglo-American aestheticians, most of whom have been oddly content to leave the question of the value of art offstage somewhere, discretely out of sight. Nor does Collingwood shy away from the ethical implications of his position. A 'philosophy of art', he says in the preface to *Principles*, has 'practical consequences bearing on the way in which we ought to approach the practice of art … and hence, because a philosophy of art is a theory as to the place of art in life as a whole, the practice of life' (*PA*, p.vii). Thus, for Collingwood, a proper understanding of art forms part of the answer to that most fundamental of ethical questions, how ought one to live? – a part he seeks to make explicit at the end of the book. I hope, here, to explain what sort of contribution to answering that question he thinks an understanding of art can make. By highlighting the ethical dimension of his thought, moreover, I hope also to suggest why his philosophy of art may be no less timely now than it was when *Principles* was first published, in 1938.

Before beginning, though, I should mention and explain an interpretative choice I have made. Just as the projects of most aestheticians have been driven by pre-existing philosophical concerns rather than artistic ones, so Collingwood, however splendidly alive to the artistic he might be, does arrive on the scene with an impressive amount of philosophical baggage, not all of it especially handy for his philosophy of art. So one is faced with an alternative: either present his aesthetics in such a way as to shed light on Collingwood's own philosophical development; or present his aesthetics in such a way as to bring out what seems most striking and valuable in it for the understanding of art, even if this does occasionally mean treating his specifically philosophical baggage with less reverence than he might have wished. I have chosen the latter course.

Collingwood's prior philosophical commitments some-times lead him, in my view, to express deep and important points about art in a quite spectacularly unhelpful way. So for the most part I've soft-pedalled them, in the belief that the depth and significance of his actual aesthetics will emerge more clearly as a result. By these means it should be possible to go to the heart of the matters that matter more directly – without, I hope, misrepresenting Collingwood unduly along the way.

1. THE CORRUPTION OF CONSCIOUSNESS

At the very end of *The Principles of Art* Collingwood makes explicit the ethical burden of his aesthetics. The artist, he says, must be a prophet: he

> must prophesy not in the sense that he foretells things to come, but in the sense that he tells his audience, at the risk of their displeasure, the secrets of their own hearts ... The reason why they need him is that no community altogether knows its own heart; and by failing in this knowledge a community deceives itself on the one subject concerning which ignorance means death ... Art is the community's medicine for the worst disease of mind, the corruption of consciousness.
>
> (*PA*, p.336)

Art, then, offers a remedy for a serious ethical condition that Collingwood calls the 'corruption of consciousness'. This is a grand claim, not to say an apocalyptic one. It is also, on the face of it at least, rather a bleak claim. One gets little sense from it that art can be a source of pleasure or diversion, or that, for most of us, the therapeutic effects of art have more to do with fending off boredom than catastrophe. For Collingwood, though, it seems that art is a medicine against death.

So what is this terrible 'disease of mind' that art is apparently to cure? The short answer is: a failure to get clear about what one thinks or feels, a failure described by Collingwood (in unhelpfully Humean terms) as the botched or aborted attempt to convert impressions into ideas. Impressions, on this account, are the brute deliverances of sense, whether outer (sensations of the external world) or inner (sensations of internal disturbance). Ideas are then the images of these brought to consciousness; or, perhaps more accurately, ideas are the result of that transformative activity of consciousness whereby impressions are made available to thought. On this model, then, the mind is sharply divided into what Collingwood calls a 'psychical' level, populated by mere inchoate impressions, and what he calls a 'conscious' or 'imaginative' level, the level of ideas; and it is in the transformation of the psychical into the imaginative that consciousness can fail or be corrupt.

This is a disastrous way for Collingwood to have put what he meant. To take his model of mind literally, after all, would be to make the very idea of a transformative failure unintelligible. An impression is, by definition, something unconverted, something not yet available to thought. Therefore it is not, and could not be, available for comparison (in thought) with the idea into which it has allegedly been converted. Therefore there is no way of deciding whether consciousness has performed its transformative function successfully or not. But if talk of success and failure is out of place, then so, emphatically, must be talk of a failure so severe as to amount to 'corruption'. Therefore it makes no sense to speak of the corruption of consciousness. That Collingwood lays himself open to such an easy objection is a sure sign that his philosophical baggage has got in the way of what he wants to say.

What he does want to say becomes clearer only when he attempts to describe the process of 'conversion' breaking down:

First, we direct our attention towards a certain feeling, or become conscious of it. Then we take fright at what we have recognized: not because the feeling, as an impression, is an alarming impression, but because the idea into which we are converting it proves an alarming idea. We cannot see our way to dominate it, and shrink from persevering in the attempt. We therefore give it up, and turn our attention to something less intimidating ... I call this the 'corruption' of consciousness; because consciousness permits itself to be bribed or corrupted in the discharge of its function, being distracted from a formidable task towards an easier one.

(*PA*, p.217)

So it turns out that we are not really dealing with a failure of conversion at all. On Collingwood's account, it seems, the impression *is* converted into an idea, and it is the idea that we shy away from. So perhaps what we have instead is a failure to complete the process of conversion. But even this doesn't seem quite right, not least since the notion of partial conversion would appear to require that one and the same thing be simultaneously an impression and an idea, a possibility surely ruled out by Collingwood's own sharp division between the psychical and the imaginative. No,

5

what seems to be going on is rather a failure to get the idea clear or fully worked out, a dishonourably motivated ducking of a certain sort of hard work. And if this is right, as I think it is, it follows that the failures that Collingwood is interested in happen, not at some mysterious intersection between impressions and ideas, but solidly in the realm of ideas themselves. What he envisages as the transformation of a psychical item into an imaginative one actually requires no reference to the 'psychical' at all.

But the transformation at issue is none the less real for that. Collingwood remarks at one point that an idea is no mere 'dress made to fit' an impression (*PA*, p.244), but is different from it in kind; and this, if one subtracts the unhelpful terminology, is surely exactly right. A clear thought is not merely an unclear one dolled up; or, to put it another way, a muddle clarified isn't just another sort of muddle: it is no sort of muddle at all. To clarify is, in that sense, to transform, and such transformations can plainly be difficult, unwelcome and even painful. The work of 'consciousness' that Collingwood is interested in, then, is the work of getting clear about one's own thoughts and feelings, of transforming muddle into clarity; and the sorts of failures that concern him are, in that sense, failures of self-knowledge.

Collingwood places an enormously high valuation on self-knowledge, for two closely related sets of reasons. The first, rather Spinozistic set, has to do with feeling or emotion. Mere feelings – i.e. feelings about which we're not clear – tend, because we have not understood them, to affect our lives in ways over which we have little control: we are at their mercy. We must, therefore, fix 'our attention on the very feeling which threatens to dominate us, and so learn to dominate it' (*PA*, p.218). We must, in other words, clarify our own feelings to ourselves and so 'convert' them into what Collingwood calls 'emotions': into feelings 'dominated or domesticated by consciousness' (*PA*, p.217). (Odd metaphors, these: domination and domestication suggest a kind of defeat or trimming down of feeling, which Collingwood certainly doesn't intend. A feeling that has been 'converted' is, for him, and as will become clear, a feeling that has been endowed with meaning, i.e. a feeling that has gained rather than lost by the process.) If we succeed in converting feelings into emotions, we free ourselves from their tyranny, and so, by an increase in self-knowledge, enjoy an increased capacity for self-government. The second advantage of self-knowledge has to do with thought. 'Unless consciousness does its work successfully,' he says, '... the very wells of truth are poisoned.' We must, in other words, if we are not 'to build on a quicksand' (*PA*, p.284), be ruthlessly honest with ourselves in our thoughts. And, again, success in this enterprise promises an increased capacity for self-government. A properly functioning consciousness, then, is a consciousness devoted to the service of self-knowledge. It is a consciousness as little at the mercy of confused thought and thoughtless feeling as possible.

A 'false' or corrupt consciousness, by contrast, is one which, because it fails to clarify its thoughts and feelings, refuses to acknowledge its own experiences as its own: it says about them ' "That ... is not mine" ' (*PA*, p.216), so that the picture it paints for itself 'of its own experience is not only a selected picture (that is, a true one so far as it goes), it is a bowdlerized picture, or one whose omissions are falsifications' (*PA*, p.218). Collingwood relates these bowdlerizations explicitly to phenomena that psychoanalysts have described 'in their own way':

> The disowning of experiences they call repression; the ascription of these to other persons, projection; their consolidation into a mass of experience, homogeneous in itself ... dissociation; and the building up of a bowdlerized experience which we will admit to be our own, fantasy-building.

> (*PA*, pp.218–19)

But he refuses to regard the symptoms of a corrupt consciousness as simply clinical; nor yet is he willing to regard them as merely moral. 'As compared with disease,' he says, 'they are more like vice; as compared with vice, they are more like disease' (*PA*, p.220). And he makes the same point when he rejects the suggestion that the falsifications of a corrupt consciousness can be classed either as 'errors' or as 'lies':

> The untruthful consciousness, in disowning certain features of its own experience, is not making a bona fide mistake, for its faith is not good; it is shirking something which its business is to face. But it is not concealing the truth, for there is no truth which it knows and is concealing. Paradoxically, we may say that it is deceiving itself; but this is only a clumsy attempt to explain what is happening within a single consciousness on the analogy of what may happen as between one intellect and another.

> (*PA*, p.219)

(In a footnote he adds: 'The untruthful consciousness is, I suppose, what Plato means [by] "the lie in the soul".')

Neither moral nor medical, then, the corruption of consciousness is perhaps best described in the words I used earlier: it is an ethical condition – ethical to the extent that one *ought* not to be like that (the sense of 'corruption' that relates it to 'vice' and to 'lies'), yet a condition to the extent that one's being like that represents a certain sort of calamity (the sense of 'corruption' that ties it to 'disease' and to 'error').

The failure to get one's thoughts and feelings clear, then, results in the alienation of oneself from one's own experiences; and intuitively, at least, it is not hard to agree that such a condition might be undesirable. But Collingwood, as we have seen – and despite his occasional insistence that for most people, for most of the time, corruption represents only a 'partial and temporary' lapse (*PA*, p.283) – thinks it much worse than that. Corruption means 'death', it is 'the worst disease of mind'; indeed it is a 'sheer or undifferentiated evil' (*PA*, p.220) in whose grip 'Moral ideals are castles in the air. Political and economic systems are cobwebs. Even common sanity and bodily health are no longer secure' (*PA*, pp.284–5). And this is bound to seem an overstatement. In part, no doubt, the tenor of Collingwood's rhetoric is a product of the circumstances under which he was writing. The rise of European fascism in the 1930s seemed to him symptomatic of an actual epidemic of corrupt consciousness. Not only in Germany, Italy or Spain, but in Britain too, people were being swept along on a wave of 'undomesticated' feeling to adopt, from the mouths of demagogues, thoughts not truly their own. Civilization itself was threatened; and so Collingwood thundered against corruption. But what he actually says about it does not, by itself, tell us enough to justify his tone. We need to be told more.

2. ART AND CRAFT

And so we turn to art. Art, remember, is meant to be 'the community's medicine for the ... corruption of consciousness'. So we might expect that it would be in Collingwood's philosophy of art that the clarification of the problem to which art is supposed to be the solution will be found. In this and the next three sections I will try to show how far that expectation is borne out.

The first third of *Principles* is devoted to an attack on what Collingwood calls the 'technical' theory of art, the apparently commonsensical view that works of art function, instrumentally, as means to various kinds of end. So, for instance, a technical theorist might suggest that art is intended to provide entertainment, or instruction, or edification. But to understand art in this way, Collingwood claims, is to confuse art with craft; it is to conflate a distinction absolutely fundamental to his aesthetics. He characterizes the differences between art and craft in six ways, of which the three most important are:

a) The means/end distinction. Craft, he says, 'always involves a distinction between means and ends, each clearly understood as something distinct from the other ...' The means are 'passed through or traversed in order to reach the end, and are left behind when the end is reached' (*PA*, p.15). Thus, the means employed by a blacksmith for making a horseshoe – hammering the iron, say – are conceptually distinct from the horseshoe he makes; and once the shoe is made, the means by which it was produced play no further part in determining whether, as a horse-shoe, the finished product is a success. Thus the blacksmith's activity is a craft. Art, by contrast, need involve no such tidy separation between means and ends. Collingwood's own example here is not ideally incisive. He considers a poet. The poet may, he grants, 'get paper and pen, fill the pen, sit down and square his elbows', and, superficially at least, these actions may appear to shadow the blacksmith's. But the poet's 'actions are preparatory not to composition (which may go on in the poet's head) but to writing' (*PA*, p.20). One sees what Collingwood means. But his point can be brought out better if one simply notes that, while a blacksmith cannot make a horseshoe without a hammer, there is nothing, beyond an ability to compose poetry, that a poet needs in order to compose a poem. In this sense, there is nothing analogous in the poet's activity to the readily identifiable means employed by the blacksmith. The poet needs no tools.

b) The planning/execution distinction. The craftsman 'knows what he wants to make before he makes it', and knows precisely: 'If a person sets out to make a table, but conceives the table only vaguely, as somewhere between two by four feet and three by six ... he is no craftsman' (*PA*, pp.15–16). The artist, by contrast, need have no particularly clear plan that he intends to execute. Imagine that a sculptor 'were simply playing about with clay, and found the clay under his fingers turning into a little dancing man'. Surely this might be a work of art, despite the fact that 'it was done without being planned in advance' (*PA*, p.22). Collingwood acknowledges the obvious fact that most art, including the best art, certainly does involve an element of planning; his point is only that, since some art need not, the distinction between planning and execution cannot be essential to art in the way that it is essential to craft.

c) The raw material/finished product distinction. Craft consists in the transformation of raw material into a finished product, the raw material being 'found ready made before the special work of the craft begins' (*PA*, p.16). 'A smith makes a horseshoe … out of a certain piece of iron, cut off a certain bar.' He does not make it, as Collingwood puts it, 'out of all the iron there is' (*PA*, p.23). A craftsman, then, has his materials to hand; and from the materials he has, he selects some and rearranges them into the finished product of his craft. The poet, by contrast, begins only with all the words there are, or with all the words he knows; and these words 'were never before his mind as a whole and in an order different from that of the poem, out of which he shuffled them till the poem, as we have it, appeared' (*PA*, p.23). Thus words cannot be construed as the poet's raw materials as pieces of iron can be construed as the blacksmith's.

According to Collingwood, the technical theory of art, which suppresses these differences, simply misses what is distinctive of art, and treats art instead as a form of craft. So the technical theory conceives the artist as employing means to achieve ends, as executing pre-existing plans in order to transform raw materials into particular finished products. And in each of these respects, he maintains, the technical theory is mistaken.

Collingwood's position is plausible, I think – but only if one bears in mind what the point of his distinctions between art and craft actually is. And this is rather easily missed. It might be thought tempting, for instance, to reel off some counter-examples, especially when they seem so easy to find. Against the first alleged difference one might suggest, say, that Michelangelo's chisel stands in much the same means/end relation to his statue of David as the blacksmith's hammer stands to a horseshoe; against the second, that Michelangelo clearly planned the statue before he executed it (the original block of marble was unusually shallow, and Michelangelo's design evidently takes this into account); and against the third, that the block of marble that Michelangelo started with is obviously the raw material which was transformed into the finished product we see today. But Collingwood can accept these counter-examples with equanimity. His concern at this point of *Principles* is entirely negative: he is not claiming that art, unlike craft, never involves distinctions between means and ends, between planning and execution, between raw material and finished product. He is claiming only that art *need* not involve these, whereas craft always does. Thus it is Collingwood who is in the business of producing counter-examples – counter-examples to the technical theory of art: 'we need only show that there are admitted examples of art to which it does not apply' to show that the theory is false (*PA*, p.29). And, if we can be brought to agree that there are such exceptions, we will be obliged to concede two points. First, that art is something different from craft; and, second, that insofar as the distinctions highlighted by the technical theory are essential to the concept of 'craft', the concept of 'art' differs from the concept of 'craft' in precisely those respects. This is all that he wishes to establish. He is not at this stage, as he makes clear in his discussion of the planning/execution distinction, offering any substantive characterization of art: he is, he says, highlighting 'a merely negative characteristic, not a positive one ... If unplanned works of art are possible [e.g. the 'little dancing man'], it does not follow that no planned work is a work of art' (*PA*, p.22). And equally, if composition without means or raw materials is possible (as it is in the poet's case), it does not follow that no work which is the result of means brought to bear on raw materials is a work of art.

Collingwood was keen not to be misunderstood on this point for another reason too. In rejecting the positive claims of the technical theory – that art, like craft, is to be grasped in terms of the instrumental distinctions discussed above – he realized that people were likely to assume that he was rejecting technique itself, that they would impute to him 'the sentimental notion that works of art can be produced by anyone, however little trouble he has taken to learn his job, provided his heart is in the right place' (*PA*, p.26). This notion he of course rejects, and he goes to some lengths to dissociate himself from it. He emphasizes 'what every artist knows':

> the vast amount of intelligent and purposeful labour, the painful and conscientious self-discipline, that has gone to the making of a man who can write a line as Pope writes it, or knock a single chip off a single stone like Michelangelo.

> (*PA*, pp.26–7)

So Collingwood is again committed only to a negative claim: that an artist's hard-won technique, to the extent that this is to be understood instrumentally (in terms of means and ends etc.), is not the essence of his art. He is not committed to the silly claim that technique is irrelevant to the production of works of art.

It follows from Collingwood's discussion of the technical theory that one should not expect his distinction between art and craft to be a distinction between two separate sets of objects. And nor is it: he points out repeatedly that one and the same object may be both a work of craft and a work of art. Indeed, insofar as most of the things we would call art are clearly the products of technique, there must be very little art that isn't also craft. The distinction is rather between the various aspects that an object may have. In its aspect as a piece of craft, the object can be understood wholly in instrumental terms: it is the end-product of means brought to bear on a certain sort of raw material in the execution of a preconceived plan. If the object also has an aspect as art, however, then – in ways yet to be specified – its point or significance goes beyond anything that can be captured in the merely instrumental characterizations appropriate to craft.

It is important to bear this point in mind if some of the things that Collingwood goes on to say are not to seem outlandish or worse, not least since he sometimes expresses himself in misleading ways. He distinguishes, for instance, between art 'properly' so-called and art 'falsely' so-called, a distinction which looks for all the world like a distinction between objects rather than aspects. And when he employs this distinction in an effort to discredit particular manifestations of the technical theory of art, the impression can strengthen. He is concerned to deny, for example, that art properly so-called has anything to do with representation. To set out to represent something, he says, is to execute a plan. It is to seek to produce a likeness in accordance with a preconceived idea of what the finished product should look like. To this extent, the task of representation is a purely technical task; and to the extent that the task is technical is a part, not of art, but of craft. One might easily read this as a denial of the claim that a representational painting can be a work of art. Or, to put it another way, one might easily read this as the claim that a representational object is, necessarily, a craft-object, and is only that. But this is not what Collingwood means:

> The view that art proper is not representative … does not imply that art and representation are incompatible. As in the case of art and craft, they overlap. A building or a cup, which is primarily an artifact or product of craft, may be also a work of art; but what makes it a work of art is different from what makes it an artifact. A representation may be a work of art; but what makes it a representation is one thing, what makes it a work of art is another.
>
> (*PA*, p.43)

So the distinction that Collingwood wants to draw is not between craft-objects and art-objects, but between respects in which an object can be seen as a piece of craft, in the sense that it can be understood instrumentally, and respects in which it can not. To the extent that an object is merely a technically executed likeness, it lacks an art-aspect; but that doesn't mean that one and the same object cannot have both a craft- and an art-aspect. Precisely the same points apply to Collingwood's rejection of what he calls 'stimulus-and-reaction' theories (*PA*, p.30), theories which regard it as the function of art to produce certain states of mind in its audience. Understood thus, of course, art is merely instrumental: it consists in the deployment of techniques to realize particular preconceived ends. It is craft. Collingwood doesn't deny that works of art *can* be amusing, uplifting, fortifying or whatever, and can be so deliberately. His point is only that their success in performing this function is not what makes them works of art.

The purpose of the art/craft distinction, then, is negative. It is to distinguish between those aspects of an object that can be understood instrumentally, as the products of technique alone, and those aspects that can't. The aspects that can't are what Collingwood means by 'art'. We don't yet know what positive characteristics 'art', in Collingwood's sense, might be supposed to have. Nor are we yet a lot closer to understanding how art might be said to be a remedy for the corruption of consciousness. Indeed, if anything, we are further away. To be a remedy, after all, is typically to be an instrument of a certain kind – it is to meet the preconceived end of curing the condition for which it is prescribed. And art, on Collingwood's view, cannot be understood instrumentally. I return to this apparently stark tension in his position in section 6.

3. THE SO-CALLED IDEAL THEORY

First, though, I must say something about an aspect of Collingwood's thought that has spawned more confusion, perhaps, than any other, a confusion that springs, I think, from an underestimation of the weight of his pre-existing philosophical baggage, together with a misconstruction of the character of his opposition to the technical theory of art. It is very regularly said that Collingwood believes that works of art, properly understood, exist only as imaginings in the artist's head, and that the external manifestations of these, on canvas (if paintings), in sound (if pieces of music), in stone (if sculptures), in words (if poems), are merely secondary and inessential versions of the real things, generously but dispensably made available by the artist to an audience. To confuse a work of art proper (the one in the artist's head) for the publicly available manifestation of it is, on this view, to mistake art for craft: the publicly available canvas (say) is merely the instrumentally executed externalization of the painting which the painter imagined before he got anywhere near a canvas or brush. The art in his head is the plan that he follows; the painting itself is just a piece of craft. This view, when attributed to Collingwood, as it almost always is, is called the Ideal Theory of art, an expression he never himself uses.

One can see, just about, why Collingwood is thought to have subscribed to the Ideal Theory. Indeed I have already touched on a couple of the reasons. For instance, if one mistakes his rejection of the third of the technical theory's claims – that art, like craft, always involves a distinction between raw material and finished product – for the counter-claim that art *never* involves such a distinction, it is possible to conclude that Collingwood regarded the role in art of publicly accessible materials, whether raw or not, as nil. And the push towards that conclusion may be increased if one also misreads his rejection of the technical theory as the rejection of technique itself: technique, after all, is detectable, if it is detectable anywhere, only in the publicly available manifestations of the artist's work. Put these two together, and the view that nothing that is the result of technique brought to bear on publicly accessible materials can be art seems to follow directly. Collingwood must have thought that art 'properly' so-called exists only in people's heads. But this conclusion, as I say, and for reasons set out in the previous section, rests on a clear misreading of Collingwood's position.

There are, however, other reasons for attributing the Ideal Theory to him, most of them lurking in the chapter of *Principles* called 'Art and Imagination'. This is the chapter in which the tendency of Collingwood's prior philosophical commitments to make him make important points about art in hopelessly misleading ways is most marked. The following statement is a particularly clear example:

> the music, the work of art, is not the collection of noises, it is the tune in the composer's head. The noises made by the performers, and heard by the audience, are not the music at all; they are only means by which the audience, if they listen intelligently ... can reconstruct for themselves the imaginary tune that existed in the composer's head.
>
> (*PA*, p.139)

And there's a fair amount more in that vein. Small wonder, then, if Collingwood is said to have thought that works of art are private, purely imaginary entities in people's heads.

Suppose for a moment that Collingwood does believe what he here appears to be saying. What would be wrong with it? The short answer is: lots, but I'll highlight only one of the many problems he would face. To think, as he appears to, that a work of art might exist solely in someone's head – that it need never receive external embodiment as a public art *object* – is to ignore the absolutely fundamental role played in the production of art by artistic media. It is only when the artist actually sets about his marble with his chisel, or addresses his canvas with his brush and his paints, that his work as an artist has begun. And the consequence of this is that the medium of his work (marble, paint, whatever) is an ineliminable part of the art he produces. Furthermore, the manner in which he *handles* his medium is very often a major source of whatever value or interest his work has: one could not, for instance, fully appreciate Van Gogh's *Self-Portrait* of 1887 without appreciating the short, stabbing brush-strokes with which he has painted the hair and the face. But none of these facts can possibly be captured by an account that insists that works of art are things in people's heads. In that sense, the Ideal Theory isn't a theory of art at all.

So what is Collingwood up to? The first thing to say is that he certainly isn't in the business of denying the importance of artistic media or of artists' interactions with them. The following passage makes this clear:

> What one paints is what can be painted; no one can do more; and what can be painted must stand in some relation to the muscular activity of painting it … Hold your pencil vertical to the paper … don't stroke the paper, dig into it; think of it as if it were the surface of a slab of clay in which you were going to cut a relief, and of your pencil as a knife.

(PA, pp.144–5)

Nor is this an isolated claim. Language, for instance, is the medium of poetic expression; but 'Take away the language, and you take away what is expressed' (*PA*, p.244), which is to say, you take away the poem. There can, then, be no art in the absence of the medium proper to it. Collingwood also accommodates the Van Gogh case: his denial that the 'means' of art are always 'passed through or traversed in order to reach the end, and are left behind when the end is reached' (*PA*, p.15), is precisely an acknowledgement of the continuing significance in many works of art of the processes by which they were made. The short, stabbing brush-strokes that Van Gogh used to paint his self-portrait weren't somehow passed beyond when the painting was finished: they are *in* the painting, indeed they are what the painting *is*. So Collingwood is fully alive to the importance of artistic media.

Why, then, does he speak as if works of art enjoyed some

20

sort of purely mental existence? The most general answer is: because Collingwood comes to his philosophy of art already convinced that *everything* enjoys a purely mental existence. Collingwood was an Idealist. He believed that the world around us is constituted by the thoughts we have about it; that to exist and to be conceived of are one and the same thing. From this point of view it is no surprise that works of art are said to exist as thoughts in people's heads, since that is just to say that works of art exist. But equally, from this point of view, the *media* of art enjoy a purely mental form of existence; and so there is no contradiction in Collingwood's insisting both that works of art are things in people's heads and that they are necessarily mediated (in language, paint, stone, or whatever). Seen in this context, Collingwood is not making a special and bizarre claim about works of art in particular, he is making a much bigger and even more bizarre claim about reality in general. And it is this claim – this major item of his philosophical baggage – that accounts for his often disconcertingly mentalistic way of putting things.

For many purposes one could draw a line under the discussion of the so-called Ideal Theory here. Collingwood was an Ideal Theorist about art because he was an Ideal Theorist about everything; so in order to understand what he is saying about art (assuming we are not Idealists ourselves), we need merely bracket off his metaphysics and regard 'thing in the head' as an eccentric way of saying 'thing in the world'. But if we did simply draw the line there, we would miss out on an important part of what Collingwood is getting at. For the remark I quoted earlier – the one about pieces of music not being collections of noises, but tunes in people's heads – is not only a restatement of Collingwood's Idealist metaphysics. It is also part of a positive point he wants to make about the experience of art.

Collingwood's point, essentially, is that to experience a work of art with understanding is to engage in a certain sort of activity with respect to it; it is to make a certain sort of effort. It is not, as some have had it, to absorb passively whatever merely sensory experiences the work of art offers. The crucial distinction that Collingwood is making, then, is between a brute series of noises (as might be perceived by a cat, say) and the piece of music heard by a person who understands those noises *as* music (cats don't hear music). It is thus the music itself that audiences who listen 'intelligently' use their 'imaginations' to 'reconstruct'. The way that Collingwood expresses this point is still uncomfortably mentalistic; but that he means what I have suggested becomes clearer a little further on:

> what we get out of [a] concert is something other than the noises made by the performers. In each case, what we get out of it is something ... which remains forever inaccessible to a person who cannot or will not make efforts of the right kind, however completely he hears the sounds that fill the room in which he is sitting.

(*PA*, p.141)

Merely to hear the sounds that fill the room would be to be like a cat. It would not be to have a musical experience. And he relates this point explicitly to the question of understanding when he discusses the experience of a lecture:

> We hear the sound of [the lecturer's] voice; but what he is doing is not simply to make noises, but to develop a scientific thesis ... The lecture, therefore, is not a collection of noises made by the lecturer with his organs of

speech; it is a collection of scientific thoughts related to those noises in such a way that a person who not only hears but thinks as well becomes able to think those thoughts for himself ... [It is] something we have to reconstruct in our own minds.

(*PA*, pp.140–1)

Collingwood's talk of 'things in the head', then, is not simply an expression of his general Idealism; it is an expression of the crucial distinction between understanding something and not understanding it. One has a scientific thesis or a piece of music 'in one's head', in Collingwood's sense, once one has made a successful effort to understand what one is hearing.

So the experience of art is not merely a passive reception of sensory stimuli. It is a species of imaginative engagement. And this fact, he suggests, accounts for much of the richness that aesthetic experiences may have. The experience of music, like that of a lecture, goes far beyond the merely acoustic; the experience of painting 'does not belong to sight alone, it belongs also (and on some occasions even more essentially) to touch' (*PA*, p.146). Indeed, as he rather thornily puts it, 'we may go so far as to call it an imaginative experience of total activity' (*PA*, p.148), a phrase whose point becomes clearer, I think, when one reads the following (characteristically brilliant) description of Cézanne, who painted 'like a blind man':

His still-life studies ... are like groups of things that have been groped over with the hands ... So with his interiors; the spectator finds himself bumping about those rooms, circumnavigating with caution those menacingly angular tables, coming up to the persons that so massively occupy those chairs and fending them

23

off with his hands. It is the same when Cézanne takes us into the open air ... A bridge is no longer a pattern of colour ... it is a perplexing mixture of projections and recessions, over and round which we find ourselves feeling our way as one can imagine an infant feeling its way ... And over the landscape broods the obsession of Mont Sainte-Victoire, never looked at, but always felt, as the child feels the table over the back of its head.

(*PA*, p.144)

This is fully of a piece with the Collingwood who insists that you should 'dig into' your paper with your pencil 'as if it were the surface of a slab of clay'. Indeed the audience's imaginative experience of the artist's imaginative engagement with his medium underwrites the very possibility of artistic communication:

When he painted [the picture, the artist] was in possession of an experience ... more or less like that which we construct for ourselves when we look at the picture. If he knew how to paint, and if we know how to look at a painting, the resemblance between this imaginary experience of his and the imaginary experience which we get from looking at his work is at least as close as that between the colours he saw in the picture and those we see; perhaps closer ... We bring our powers of vision with us, and find what they reveal. Similarly, we bring our imaginative powers with us, and find what they reveal: namely, an imaginary experience of total activity which we find in the picture because the painter had put it there.

(*PA*, pp.149–51)

Through the veil of Collingwood's Idealism, this passage,

like the last three I have quoted, makes genuine and valuable points about art and the experience of it, none of them even remotely compatible with the belief that art 'properly' so-called, being something in the head, is logically and ontologically cut off from the mediated, publicly accessible objects encountered in the concert hall, studio or gallery.

To the question, then, Was Collingwood an Ideal Theorist? two sorts of answer are possible. In a global sense the answer is yes: art, like everything else, including the publicly accessible media of its embodiment, is real for him to the extent that it is constituted in our thoughts. But in any sense having specifically to do with art, the answer is no: both artist and audience have access to the same embodied work of art, and have access to it in the same way. The failure to keep these two issues separate from one another (a failure that is partly Collingwood's own) has, not unexpectedly, resulted in some strange interpretations of his thought. But I hope I have said enough here to suggest that Collingwood's global Idealism is really only a distraction from the much more important and interesting ideas that constitute his aesthetics.

4. EXPRESSION

We are now in a position to make sense of Collingwood's main positive thesis about art, a thesis which draws on both his rejection of the technical theory and his insistence on the significance of the artist's 'imaginative' engagement with his medium. The thesis also provides the bridge to Collingwood's ethical worries about the corruption of consciousness. It can be stated swiftly. Collingwood claims that art is expression.

But he means something rather particular by 'expression'. He distinguishes sharply between expressing an emotion and betraying an emotion. To betray an emotion is to exhibit its symptoms. Someone betrays his fear if 'he turns pale and stammers', his anger if 'he turns red and bellows; and so forth' (*PA*, p.121). These exhibitions of emotions are, Collingwood grants, often, in ordinary talk, called 'expressions'. But he is interested in a more restricted sense of the term, a sense – he calls it expression 'proper' – which shadows the sense of art when it is 'properly' so-called. This restricted sense consists, not merely in making it clear that one is in a certain sort of state, as the betrayal of emotion does, but in making clear just *what* that state is. To begin with, says Collingwood, the person engaged in expression knows next to nothing of what he feels:

> All he is conscious of is a perturbation or excitement, which he feels going on within him, but of whose nature he is ignorant. While in this state, all he can say about his emotion is 'I feel ... I don't know what I feel.' From this helpless and oppressed condition he extricates himself by doing something which we call expressing himself.
>
> (*PA*, p.109)

The process of extrication is the process of answering the question, What *is* it I feel? At the beginning of the process there simply is no answer to that question: one's state is inchoate. At the end of the process, however, there is an answer, and it is given in the expression one comes up with. Expression, then, is the activity of getting clear about one's own experience, an activity which transforms the experience as it clarifies it. One's experience is thus fully and completely distinctive only once expression is itself complete. 'Until a man has expressed his emotion, he does not yet know what emotion it is' (*PA*, p.111). Hence 'the expression of emotion is not' something 'made to fit an emotion already existing, but is an activity without which the experience of that emotion cannot exist' (*PA*, p.244). So an emotion is not revealed for what it is through being expressed: it becomes what it is through being expressed.

On Collingwood's construction, then, it is clear that there can be no genuine distinction between the emotion expressed and the expression of it. And this is significant. It means, for instance, that the emotion expressed is always, and of necessity, mediated. One may express one's experience in words or in gestures; one may express it in paint, sounds or stone. But one must always express it in *something*. So the act of expression is tied indissolubly to the medium through which it is achieved. The significance of this lies partly in the additional space it opens up between Collingwood's position and the suggestion that works of art are private things in people's heads. For if art just *is* the expression of emotion, and if expression is necessarily mediated, art too is necessarily mediated. No work of art, on this account, can be conceived of in isolation from the medium in which it is embodied. Therefore works of art exist, not in the head, but in the publicly accessible media of their embodiment. And there is a further consequence. Collingwood insists that expression is an 'exploration' of one's own experience (*PA*, p.111). But, if expression is necessarily mediated, it follows that that exploration must also be an exploration of one's medium of expression. To take Collingwood's own example: Cézanne explored his response to Mont Sainte-Victoire, in fact his obsession with it, by painting it again and again. He explored his obsession through his paint. But equally, he explored his paint through his obsession. The 'felt mass', like 'a table over the head', is not only a discovery, expressed in a particular medium, about his response to the mountain; it is also, and by the same token, a discovery about the possibilities of the medium in which the mountain is embodied. The two sides of the coin cannot be prised apart.

This is a beautiful point. It captures perfectly the intuition, shared by many aestheticians apart from Collingwood, that the medium of a work is no mere vehicle for the art in it, but is an inseparable part of the art. This intuition can be expressed in a number of ways. Of a poem, for example, one might say that it is really as much about words as it is about what these particular words are being used to say; or, of a statue, that its real subject is as much the stone as the figure that has been carved out from it. One can see what these claims are intended to mean, more or less. But it is Collingwood's achievement, through his analysis of the essentially mediated character of expression, to have explained in what sense such claims might be true; and if his philosophy of art had done nothing but this, it would have been important enough.

But it does do more. The expression of emotion, remember, is said to be different from the betrayal of emotion in that expression, unlike betrayal, is a process of clarification. But Collingwood also wants to make another distinction. 'If you want to express the terror that something causes,' he says,

> you must not give it an epithet like 'dreadful'. For that describes the emotion instead of expressing it ... Some people have thought that a poet who wishes to express

a great variety of subtly differentiated emotions might be hampered by the lack of a vocabulary rich in words referring to the distinctions between them ... This is the opposite of the truth. The poet needs no such words at all ... To describe a thing is to call it a thing of such and such a kind: to bring it under a conception, to classify it. Expression, on the contrary, individualizes.

(PA, p.112)

Thus, while description does clarify, in the sense that it is concerned with classification, it clarifies by generalizing. It groups a particular thing together with other things of the same general sort. Expression, by contrast, marks the distinctions, not merely between different sorts of things, but between different things that might be described in the same way. To express something, Collingwood says, is to clarify it in all its particularity:

The artist proper is a person who, grappling with the problem of expressing a certain emotion, says, 'I want to get this clear.' It is of no use to him to get something else clear, however like it this other thing may be. He does not want a thing of a certain kind, he wants a certain thing.

(PA, p.114)

Description, of course, would yield only 'a thing of a certain kind'. Expression yields the thing itself. This point, then, is a corollary of Collingwood's earlier observation that what a thing expresses is inseparable from the expression of it; or, to put it slightly differently, that what a particular work of art expresses is something unique, to be found there and nowhere else.

This, again, is immensely significant. There has been a

tendency in the philosophy of art, both before Colling-wood and since, to suppose that anything that can be expressed can also be described independently. And this supposition has been shared even by those who would accord no less importance to expression than Collingwood does. So, for instance, Leo Tolstoy, whose book *What is Art?* is a fervently expressionist tract, argues that an artist first has an emotion, that he knows what it is, and that he then sets out to design an object – the work of art – which will express it. For Tolstoy, then, and despite the evidence to the contrary furnished by his own novels, the emotion to be expressed is understood fully and independently of the expression it eventually receives. But if this were right, it would follow that two quite distinct works of art could, in principle, express precisely the same thing. Which is to say that one work of art could, in principle, be replaced by another (they would be two things of the same kind). And that, surely, is the opposite of the truth. The finale of Mozart's seventeenth piano concerto expresses exuberance; so does the finale of Beethoven's second. But the two are not interchangeable, even though they can both be described in the same terms (as exuberant); and the reason they're not interchangeable is that each expresses an exuberance that is all its own. Collingwood's distinction between expression and description is designed to make just this point.

So Collingwood's account of expression achieves at least two important things: it explains how the medium of expression is inseparable from what is expressed in it; and it explains why an expression is always unique. In doing these things, moreover, it brings home the full force of, and the thinking behind, his distinction between art and craft. Craft is a matter of matching means to the production of preconceived ends. Such ends, clearly, must be specifiable in advance, and so must be specifiable in general terms. 'However accurately defined', the end at which a craft aims 'is always defined as the production of a thing having characteristics that could be shared by other things' (*PA*, p.113). Thus it is the business of a craftsman to produce things that satisfy certain descriptions – for instance, to produce a table of given dimensions out of a particular type of material – where those descriptions could, in principle, be satisfied equally well by an indefinitely large number of other objects. There are, then, as Collingwood insists, clear distinctions in craft between means and ends and between planning and execution. Craft aims at the production of things 'of a certain kind'. It follows from this that expression cannot be a species of craft. When one sets about expressing oneself, one does not yet know what the outcome will be:

> There is certainly here a directed process: an effort, that is, directed upon a certain end; but the end is not something foreseen and preconceived, to which an appropriate means can be thought in the light of our knowledge of its special character.

> (*PA*, p.111)

– because knowledge of that 'special character' is precisely the end at which expression aims. In the relevant sense, then, one cannot 'execute' an expression in accordance with a 'plan', since to have a plan would be to know already what the 'special character' of the outcome is to be; and if one knew that, the expression would already have been executed. Nor is the emotion expressed somehow the raw material from which the expression is made, something

31

which is 'present to' a person's 'mind at the commence-
ment of his labour, and which that labour converts into' an
expression (*PA*, p.23); for until the labour is complete
neither he nor anyone else knows what emotion is to be
expressed.

A successful expression, then, a successful work of art,
stands in a quite different relation to the labour of
producing it than a successful piece of craft does. A
craftsman plans a certain end, selects the means appropriate to its execution and is held to have succeeded insofar as
a proper match has been brought off between the two. An
artist, by contrast, isn't trying to match anything with
anything. Because he lacks plans or means in the relevant
sense, his ends can be said to have been realized only in the
act of execution; and the result of his labours, the work of
art proper, is a success not if it matches up with some
preconceived description (a plan) – not, that is, if it is 'a
thing of a certain kind' – but if it counts as an expression, if
it counts as 'a certain thing'. The artist explores his medium
of expression; he feels his way; he says to himself, 'This line
won't do,' until he has got it right (*PA*, p.283). He can give
no prior specification of what the right line will be; but
when he's got it, he knows. And when he has finished, it is
because the question, What *is* it I feel? has been answered.
His answer is the expression itself.

Collingwood's thesis here, quite apart from its importance for aesthetics, is a salutary corrective to certain
standard accounts of purposeful action. According to these,
an action is purposeful – can be said to have been done for a
reason – only if the purpose or reason it serves can be
specified independently of the action itself. So, for example,
one acts purposefully when one shoots at goal in an
attempt to score. One can say what the purpose of the

action is – to get the ball to cross a particular line in accordance with the rules – without referring to just *this* shot, or to any particular shot at all. And such an analysis is no doubt perfectly adequate to the case, as it would be for many kinds of purposeful action. But that analysis is hopelessly inadequate for those other kinds of action, no less purposeful, about which one can say only: 'No, that's not quite right … try again … no … Yes! *That's* what I was after.' In cases such as this, no specification of the purpose of the action can be given without reference to the action itself; but one is acting purposefully none the less. Collingwood, not unreasonably, takes the production of art to be paradigmatic of this kind of action. But when one notes that many much more mundane activities – such as trying to say clearly what one means – are exactly similar, the scope and importance of his analysis becomes plain. And nothing that matters about this kind of action can be captured remotely by the craft-model. To the extent that art is expression, then, no amount of tinkering with the terminology of means and ends, of planning and execution, will do justice to the sort of process that Collingwood is describing. Which is why he insists, in perhaps the single most penetrating sentence of the book, that 'Expression is an activity of which there can be no technique' (*PA*, p.111).

5. ART PROPER

Art proper is expression; and expression is that 'of which there can be no technique'. Collingwood speaks mostly about expressing emotions. But he makes it plain in a number of places that his account is intended to include the expression of thoughts as well (see, e.g., *PA*, pp.267–9, but beware of the philosophical baggage), so that art proper consists in the expression or clarification of both, or of either.

This has generally been taken to be Collingwood's attempt to define the concept 'art', to identify a property that all and only works of art have in common, and in virtue of which they are called art. And so, in a way, it is. But it is important to notice how very uninformative that definition is. For what it is that works of art have in common, on Collingwood's account, is the fact that they quite literally defy description. So to say of them that they belong to a class of things (i.e. to the class of artworks) – that they are, in other words, things of 'a certain kind' – is, if true, only trivially true: for each one's membership of the class is determined only by its being, in Collingwood's terms, 'a certain thing'. The seemingly essentialist definition of art proper as expression, then, works precisely to rule out the identification of anything that members of the class of artworks might informatively be said to have in common: the definition serves to discourage essentialist ambitions rather than to satisfy them.

Nor is this the only reason to be cautious about reading Collingwood's definition as an attempt to identify the essence of art. The term 'art', as I have already said, picks out for Collingwood, not a distinct class of objects, but a particular aspect that various different sorts of object may exhibit: the aspect of being an expression, of being a clarified thought or feeling. On his view, therefore, one and the same object can be both craft and art. A film-composer commissioned to write a piece of music to accompany a love scene may successfully meet his brief by composing something entirely generic (sweeping string tunes, swelling horn-notes – the works). To the extent that this describes his achievement, he has produced a piece of craft. He has produced 'a thing of a certain kind'. But he may also have done something more. His sweeping string tunes, swelling horn-notes and so on, may also constitute 'a certain thing'; they may, in other words, be a clarification in music of the composer's thoughts and feelings about love. To the extent that this is the case, he has produced a work of art. So the same object can be both; and there would be something uncomfortable, to put it no higher, about the idea of a property which both was and was not the essence of one and the same object. Certainly I doubt that there would be much point in talking about the essences of aspects. So it is perhaps no surprise, in light of this, that Collingwood nowhere claims to have defined or to have identified the essence of art.

But it will not have escaped notice that he *is* bringing off an identification of another sort: of art proper with the uncorrupt consciousness. Art, in Collingwood's view, is the expression of thoughts and feelings, where expression means clarification; and the proper job of consciousness, according to him, is the 'conversion' of muddle into clarity. So the proper job of consciousness is expression, and conversion and expression mean the same thing. It follows from this that conversion 'is an activity of which there can be no technique'. The discussion of the previous three sections should have put us in a much better position to understand the senses in which that activity might fail; to understand what Collingwood means, in other words, when he talks about the corruption of consciousness.

To put it in a nutshell: a consciousness is corrupt whenever it seeks to discharge its service to self-knowledge through technical means. It is corrupt, for instance, when it misunderstands the medium through which its work is to be done as a mere vehicle for the thought or feeling it is attempting to clarify. Conversion (i.e. expression) is essentially mediated; it consists in an 'exploration' of one's own experience; therefore, and as Collingwood brings out so vividly in his discussion of Cézanne, it consists also in an exploration of the medium in which the conversion is to be attempted. Suppose one is trying to express oneself in words. One must, if one is to succeed in clarifying one's thoughts and feelings, approach the task with as much regard and respect for the words themselves as for what one is trying to get them to say. The effort to discover what one thinks or feels, the effort to produce a clear statement, is thus inevitably also an effort to discover more about what the words one is exploring can be used to do. Just as Cézanne made discoveries about paint in painting Mont Sainte-Victoire, and succeeded in capturing his thought about the mountain only through his attentiveness to his medium, so the person who succeeds in saying what he thinks must, through his attentiveness to words, make discoveries about language. The corrupt consciousness, by contrast, regards its medium as only a vehicle, ready-made for use. It is indifferent to its special characteristics; it has no urge to explore them; and so, through a certain kind of disregard, debars itself from converting its muddles into clear expressions of what it thinks and feels. Its failure to engage imaginatively with its medium issues directly in a failure of self-knowledge.

To treat one's medium of conversion or expression as a mere vehicle is to treat it as a means to an end; it is to suppose that the technically appropriate manipulation of the former can be made to yield the latter. And this, if Collingwood's analysis of expression is right, is certainly to make a mistake. It is also, and by the same token, to forego the individualization of one's thoughts and feelings in favour of the classification of them. The person engaged in expression, remember, says, 'I want to get this clear.' 'It is of no use to him to get something else clear, however like it this other thing may be' (*PA*, p.114). Yet to settle for mere technique is precisely to get something else clear: it is to arrive at 'a thing of a certain kind' instead of 'a certain thing'. Rather than engage in a process whose end is reached only when one finally says, 'Yes! *That's* what I was after,' the corrupt consciousness stops the process short. It arrives at a point when it says, 'Oh, well, perhaps that's not quite what I wanted; but it'll do,' and moves on. It has no inclination to engage in the sort of exploration of its medium that would lead to a genuine expression, and contents itself instead with a vague formula that might equally apply to a whole range of subtly different thoughts or feelings. And again, the outcome is a failure of self-knowledge, a failure to follow the difficult task of expression through.

Collingwood's target, then, is a certain sort of laziness. The corrupt consciousness ducks out of the hard work of expression, so that its knowledge of itself is 'bowdlerized'. When it does this, the result is 'bad art' (*PA*, p.285). Bad art

– and this is important – is therefore possible only if there has been a prior intention to produce an expression, only if someone has first set out 'to get [something] clear' and has then shirked the task. It is not the case, therefore, that Collingwood thinks one is corrupt whenever one produces 'a thing of a certain kind'; for one may not have intended to produce anything else. One may be a craftsman, and a craftsman is not, on Collingwood's account, a failed artist: a craftsman is no sort of artist at all. Nor, I think, is Collingwood suggesting that every failure to produce 'a certain thing', when that is what is intended, constitutes corruption. For there can be different kinds of failure. The artist who says 'This line won't do' has, just at the moment, failed. But, unless he shirks the task of putting it right, his failure is not corrupt. He has not been false to the intention to 'get this clear', he has merely not yet succeeded in doing what he wanted to do. And, as with individual lines, so with complete canvases. Cézanne painted Mont Sainte-Victoire obsessively. Had he been entirely successful in clarifying his experience of the mountain the first time round, he would not, presumably, have felt driven to paint it again (and again). In that sense, many or even all of his paintings of the mountain might be failures. But they would not be corrupt failures: for the intention to 'get this clear' has never been suspended. Cézanne, relentless in his efforts to produce 'a certain thing', demonstrably refuses to settle for 'a thing of a certain kind'. Nothing is being shirked here; and his failures, if failures they are, are noble ones. The corrupt artist, by contrast, intends to 'get this clear', fails, and then misrepresents his failure to himself as success. He dishonestly regards his intention as having been fulfilled, and so, in shirking the task of going on, disowns the experience that he meant to clarify. Were one to overlook the distinction between shirking and merely, for the moment, failing, one would be obliged to attribute to Collingwood the uncompelling view, which there is no sign of his holding, that the vast majority of artworks are the failed expressions of a corrupt consciousness.

Art proper, then, on Collingwood's account, just is expression; and expression is the characteristic activity of a properly functioning consciousness. It follows from this that the label 'art proper' applies not only to the sorts of object that we would normally describe as works of art, but to any successful expression whatever, including those found in everyday acts of communication. Collingwood is keen here to draw attention to two important points, both of them still worth making: that art is continuous with the rest of life, and not sharply cut off from it; and that much of what we value in works of art (normally so-called) is really only a heightened and concentrated version of something we would value wherever we found it. Unfortunately, however, he overstates his case. At one point he even claims that 'Every utterance and every gesture that each one of us makes is a work of art' (*PA*, p.285). And that surely can't be right. It is not at all plausible to think that one should or even could intend to 'get this clear' – in Collingwood's strong sense of those words – every time one speaks or waves one's arm. For many purposes and in many contexts 'a thing of a certain kind' will do perfectly adequately, and one strives for no more (and so cannot be said to have failed, corruptly or otherwise, when 'a thing of a certain kind' is all one produces). Collingwood seems to have forgotten that the same sorts of objects can have craft-aspects as well as art-aspects, and hence that speaking and gesturing may, in the run of everyday practical life, be more appropriately seen as craft than as art. His case, properly stated, is only that speaking and gesturing *can* be art, not that they must be; and that, at least, is perfectly plausible.

6. *THE WASTE LAND*

I postponed discussion at the end of section 2 of an apparent contradiction in Collingwood's position. He claims that art is a cure for the corruption of consciousness; but he also claims that art cannot be understood instrumentally, as a means to any preconceived end. It would seem – on the face of it at least – that these claims cannot both be true. But I think we are now in a position to see that they can be. In fact from one point of view they are quite self-evidently compatible. If art is expression, and if expression (i.e. conversion) is the proper business of consciousness, then art is obviously the remedy for corruption, since it simply *is* the successful execution of the task that the corrupt consciousness fails to perform. And to say this is not to think of art instrumentally, as a means to an end. Expression is not a means to the end of solving the problem posed by corruption, since it just *is* the solution to that problem. In this sense, then, the claim that art is the cure for a corrupt consciousness comes to nothing more than the boring and empty claim that the cure for getting something wrong is getting it right. But this reading of Collingwood's position, while it eliminates any apparent tension in it, does so only because it eliminates all content.

This is not Collingwood's way of resolving the tension. His way depends, I think, on the point I mentioned a moment ago: that what we find in works of art is a heightened, intensified version of what we find in ordinary, everyday acts of expression. 'There is no distinction of kind', he says, between an artist and anyone else; the artist 'is singular' only 'in his ability to take the initiative' (*PA*, p.119), an ability founded on his unusually intense engagement with his medium. The work that he then produces, insofar as it is art (i.e. insofar as it is the product of an intention to get something clear), is not only a case of expression, it is, if successful, an exemplary case. In experiencing it, in grasping the 'certain thing' that the artist has expressed, we, the audience, are shown or reminded what it is like to get something clear, to get something right. And this experience may discourage us from ducking the task of clarifying our own thoughts and feelings. If it does discourage us, the art we experience is acting as a remedy for the corruption of consciousness. But it is doing so just insofar as we have not understood it instrumentally. The art is effective as an exemplar, in other words, only to the extent that we have not mistaken it for 'a thing of a certain kind'. And if this is right, there is no tension in Collingwood's position. Art proper has a medicinal effect against the corruption of consciousness precisely when it is not understood as a means to an end. Both of the apparently conflicting claims are true.

This again is valuable and acute. The power of exemplars to influence is notoriously difficult to articulate, as the surface tension between Collingwood's two claims suggests. But the basic machinery of his position is, as I have tried to show, of exactly the right sort to overcome the difficulty in principle. His attempt to illustrate its overcoming in practice, however, is more complex.

In producing an exemplary public expression, he says, an artist 'is treating himself and his audience in the same kind of way; he is making his emotions clear to his audience,

41

and that is what he is doing to himself' (*PA*, p.111). If we, as his audience, are able to engage imaginatively with the artist's own imaginative exploration of his medium of expression, we will understand him; and in understanding him, Collingwood claims, his emotions become ours:

> if one person says something by way of expressing what is in his mind, and another hears and understands him, the hearer who understands him has that same thing in his mind ... [And this] is equally true of expressing emotions ... [W]hen someone reads and understands a poem, he is not merely understanding the poet's expression of his, the poet's, emotions, he is expressing emotions of his own in the poet's words, which have thus become his own words. As Coleridge put it, we know a man for a poet by the fact that he makes us poets.
>
> (*PA*, p.118)

This sounds an odd thing to say. The most natural thing would be to suggest that one understood the poet's emotions, but understood them as his rather than one's own. But perhaps Collingwood is on to something. The first part of the quoted passage certainly seems right: if I fully understand a thought that someone expresses to me, there is a perfectly clear sense in which I can make that thought my own. If you explain to me a theoretical solution to a certain sort of problem, and I grasp properly what you have said, I will be able to solve problems of the same sort for myself. It would be very strange to insist that in doing so I was employing ideas that were still somehow distinctively yours. Rather, one would say, I am employing ideas that are now mine. We have them in common, we both understand them. I have, in that sense, made your thoughts my own.

If, then, it is possible to express a thought so that someone else who understands it can make it his own, why should it not be possible to express an emotion to the same effect?

The reason one may want to resist this suggestion, I suspect, is that feelings seem more private than thoughts. There is a sense, brought out by the example above, in which thoughts are public property; whereas my being in such-and-such an emotional state seems to be a fact quite peculiar to *me*, however well other people might understand how I feel. But to object in this way would be to miss Collingwood's point. He is not talking about some species of private inner disturbance when he talks about emotion. He is talking, as he puts it, about feelings 'dominated or domesticated by consciousness' (*PA*, p.217). Which is to say, he is talking about emotions that have been given expression, and have been given it in a publicly accessible medium (in words, for instance, or in paint). Emotions, on this account, have much more in common with thoughts than they have with any kind of inner disturbance. Given which, to say that someone might express 'emotions of his own in' a 'poet's words, which have thus become his own words', is not perhaps so odd after all.

This is one of the ways in which Collingwood envisages art having an effect on its audience. To the extent that we understand what an artist has done, and grasp the 'certain thing' that the artist has expressed, our thoughts and feelings are themselves transformed. This is possible for us to the extent that we 'are capable of experiencing' what the artist himself has experienced (*PA*, p.118). Which, I take it, is to say that the emotion we make our own must fit into, and so clarify, our pre-existing emotional experience, in much the way that we can only make a thought our own if it relates in appropriate ways to, and clarifies, thoughts we already have. When we succeed in grasping the 'certain thing' that an artist has expressed, we have experienced a work of art proper as an exemplary expression. But Collingwood also has something else in mind. In the sort of case I have just been talking about, the audience acquires new thoughts and feelings, which it makes its own. But the audience may also, he suggests, come to grasp thoughts and feelings which were already in some sense its own, yet which had not before been recognized or clarified.

It is in this connection that a poet may be 'a prophet'. The poet may succeed in discovering, by expressing them, not only the 'secrets' of his own heart, but also the secrets of the 'community' he addresses (*PA*, p.336). This is possible, Collingwood suggests, because no man is 'a self-contained and self-sufficient creative power'. Rather, 'in his art as in everything else', man

> is a finite being. Everything that he does is done in relation to others like himself. As artist, he is a speaker; but a man speaks as he has been taught; he speaks the tongue in which he was born ... The child learning his mother tongue ... learns simultaneously to be a speaker and to be a listener; he listens to others speaking and speaks to others listening. It is the same with artists. They become poets or painters or musicians not by some process of development from within, as they grow beards; but by living in a society where these languages are current. Like other speakers, they speak to those who understand.
>
> (*PA*, pp.316–17)

The artist's relation to his audience is therefore, as Collingwood puts it, 'collaborative' (*PA*, p.311), in the sense that the artist's speech – his art – is possible only because he and his audience constitute a community of speakers and listeners. The self-knowledge of such a community, as articulated and understood in its speaking and listening, is therefore also inherently collaborative. A 'man becomes aware of himself as a person only so far as he finds himself standing in relation to others of whom he simultaneously becomes aware as persons' (*PA*, p.317): he recognizes himself in others and others in himself. It follows from this that the self-understanding of a community may be transformed by an artist's speech. When an artist succeeds in getting something clear, he has discovered a secret about himself. His 'awareness' of himself 'as a person' has been 'reinforced, developed, applied in new ways'; and on 'every such occasion' the same 'appeal must be made: he must find others whom he can recognize as persons in this new fashion' (*PA*, p.317). Such others, if he finds them, are his audience, and, to the extent that they grasp what he says, their understanding of themselves and of the community they collectively constitute is also 'reinforced, developed, applied in new ways'. The artist's self-knowledge (i.e. his expression) is dependent on his membership of a community of speakers and listeners, then; but what he expresses may, reciprocally, allow that community to recognize itself in a 'new fashion', to acknowledge the artist's 'secrets' as its own. When this happens, the artist is 'a prophet'.

T.S. Eliot, according to Collingwood, was a prophet when he wrote *The Waste Land*. It would be pointless to try to paraphrase what he says about it:

> The decay of civilization, as depicted in *The Waste Land*, is not an affair of violence and wrong-doing ... [Rather,] it is the picture of a whole world of men, shadows themselves, flowing over London Bridge in the winter

fog of that Limbo which involves those who, because they never lived, are equally hateful to God and to his enemies ... The poem depicts a world where the wholesome flowing water of emotion, which alone fertilizes all human activity, has dried up. Passions that once ran so strongly as to threaten the defeat of prudence, the destruction of human individuality, the wreck of men's little ships, are shrunk to nothing. No one gives; no one will risk himself by sympathizing; no one has anything to control. We are imprisoned in ourselves, becalmed in a windless selfishness ... This poem ... describes an evil where no one and nothing is to blame ... a disease which has so eaten into civilization that political remedies are about as useful as poulticing a cancer.

(*PA*, pp.334–5)

These are the secrets that Eliot invites his audience, 'at risk of their displeasure', to recognize as their own (*PA*, p.336).

With respect to the corruption of consciousness, Eliot's achievement – as read by Collingwood – is complex. The poet has produced an exemplary expression. *The Waste Land*, as 'a certain thing', works against the corruption of consciousness by reminding its audience what it is like to get something right. But what Eliot has got right is not just any old thing: it is something that the audience recognizes as its own. And to get *that* right is to work against the corruption of consciousness in another way. Remember Collingwood's description of the corrupt consciousness as one that disowns its own experiences. It embarks on the process of clarification, but shies away from what it suspects it will find. It says: 'That ... is not mine' (*PA*, p.216). In order for me, as a member of the community with whom the poet is collaborating, to realize or acknowledge that he has expressed the secrets of my own heart, therefore, I must already have shied away from clarifying them. I must already have disowned them. And so, to the experience of grasping the poet's art as an exemplary expression, i.e. to the experience of making his thoughts and feelings my own, there is added the horrible thrill of recognition: not just '*That's* right!'; but 'That's *right!*' When this happens, a quite specific failure of self-knowledge is rectified. As an exemplary expression, the work of art may incite me to a predisposition against corruption as such. But as an exemplary expression of thoughts and feelings in which I recognize myself, the work of art may also bring to light the 'certain thing' which this or that episode of corruption had previously managed to 'bowdlerize'. And to succeed in this is to be 'a prophet' in the authentic sense. It is to tell the truth about what we have in common.

This, then, is what Collingwood means when he says that art can be prophetic and that, as prophecy, it can be a remedy for the corruption of consciousness. The general structure of the point does not, of course, depend upon *The Waste Land*'s succeeding in the way that Collingwood says: in structure, the point is simply an elaboration of his analysis of expression. But the temperature of Collingwood's rhetoric does depend on his reading of *The Waste Land*, I think. The failures of self-knowledge that made fascism possible were doubtless bad enough. But Collingwood's horribly bleak view of the selves whose secrets *The Waste Land* prophetically expresses (which is to say his horribly bleak view of his contemporaries, and perhaps of himself), pushes his rhetoric over the edge and his argument out of kilter. These, to him, are selves who have evaded the secrets of their own hearts so efficiently that there is, paradoxically, next to nothing left in them to evade. Having 'never lived' and so having nothing 'to control', they have nothing to disown. Or, to put the point another way, these are beings who, because they are 'imprisoned' in themselves, are members of no community at all. Self-knowledge, which depends on the recognition of oneself in others, is therefore impossible for them. Which is to say, expression is impossible for them: 'emotion' has 'dried up' and they are incapable even of forming the intention, essential to expression, 'to get [something] clear', let alone of acting on it.

The condition of these Londoners is therefore worse than mere corruption, for they are beyond it: they are without a healthy consciousness to corrupt. And this means, of course, that they entirely lack the capacity to grasp *The Waste Land* or anything else as an exemplary expression. This is not a community that could be prophesied to, because it is not a community of any sort. Which, if Collingwood's reading of the poem is right, and if the picture he finds there of his contemporaries is accurate, means that Eliot was wasting his breath. Such 'shadows' as these are unreachable. One can see why Collingwood might say that this makes them 'hateful to God and to his enemies' alike: certainly it makes them hateful to Collingwood. He inveighs against corruption, and no doubt rightly. But he wants to have it both ways: he slips from talking about the corruption of consciousness into talking about a spiritual condition so bleak that there is nothing even in it to corrupt (or to reach), and he inveighs all the more loudly against that. He calls both 'diseases', but does not notice that they are different diseases. And so, when he's in what one might call his 'hollow man' mood, he starts equating corruption with death. It is this, I think, that accounts for his tone. He has so ensnared himself in the implications of his own diagnosis that he has left himself nothing, in effect, to express; and so he thunders. Elsewhere in the book, he calls this sort of thing 'ranting' (*PA*, p.123).

But if Collingwood ends the book rather at sixes and sevens with himself, as I think he does, this detracts nothing from his overall achievement. The distinction he draws between art and craft is seminal: no one who understands it can doubt that the technical theory of art is every bit as dead as Collingwood pronounces it. His analysis of expression and of its necessarily mediated character is wholly original and, in my view, altogether compelling; it is also a deep analysis, whose lessons subsequent aestheticians have still to take fully on board. And the ethical dimension of his thought, seen most clearly in the idea of expression as exemplary remedy, is, even at its most contentious, never less than stimulating. To have brought off this much in a single book is something that no other recent aesthetician has come close to achieving. Collingwood's reflections on the principles of art will remain important, I am certain, for as long as people remain convinced that art itself is important.

AFTERWORD

I said at the beginning that *The Principles of Art* may be as timely now as it was when it was first published. I'd like finally, by way of a few remarks about the educational implications of Collingwood's analysis of art, to suggest a reason why.

Education is or should be a preparation for life. One vital

aspect of that preparation must surely be to cultivate the capacity for self-government, a capacity dependent, as Collingwood insists, upon self-knowledge. There used to be a reasonably widespread grasp of the difference between education – often called 'academic' education – and vocational training, the difference being that vocational training, unlike education, is technical. The trainee is taught skills and techniques useful for realizing preconceived ends of various kinds. The trainee is taught crafts; and of course this is valuable. No one doubts that. But education is something different. Education has to do with self-knowledge. The student is introduced to books, ideas, theories, works of art, formulae; not in the hope, primarily, that they might prove to be useful later, as ways of getting things done, but in the hope that they will be understood. To understand, to grasp fully what a poem, a theory in physics or a historical treatise *means* is to grasp it as the precise articulation of a particular thought. It is to understand how it might differ from the articulation of closely similar thoughts. It is, in Collingwood's sense, to make the thought, as 'a certain thing', one's own, to experience it as an exemplary expression. Someone who does this learns both what precision is *like* and also, by the same token, how very imprecise he has been accustomed to be. This may induce a certain intolerance towards imprecision on his own part in the future; and, if it does, education has taken place. Understanding the thoughts expressed by others thus enhances one's capacity to get clear about one's own thoughts; and self-knowledge underwrites self-government. The value of an encounter with the thoughts of others, then, lies in the refusal to regard the encounter instrumentally. When it is properly so-called, education is aesthetic; it is something 'of which there can be no technique'.

All of this used to be well understood. But not any more, or at least not in 'higher' education as it is practised in Britain today. Unclear political thinking, together with a craven acceptance of it by people who really ought to know better, has led to the pernicious doctrine that education, if it is to be worthwhile, must impart something called 'transferable skills'. This is what Collingwood would have called the technical theory of education. The point of education on this account is to teach means that can be applied to ends that are specifiable in advance. It is no longer enough that a student should grapple with and attempt to understand a difficult book or idea, or that, through his encounters with exemplary articulations of thought and feeling, a student should come to prize clarity for its own sake. Instead he must develop impossible skills – understanding 'skills', articulation 'skills', clarity 'skills' – none of which exists, because none of them is a craft. All of them, however, are supposed to be both teachable and transferable to domains having nothing to do with the books and ideas the student has grappled with. The difference between getting 'a certain thing' right and getting 'a thing of a certain kind' right is abolished; and so the distinction between education and vocational training collapses.

None of this would matter if the ideology of transferable skills were just the hobby-horse of some fringe set of educationalists. But it does matter very much when that ideology is the official ideology, when the funding, and even the existence, of educational institutions is dependent on satisfying the government's 'quality assessors' that transferable skills are indeed being taught. Under these conditions, which are the conditions obtaining in Britain today, the effect is to drive education properly so-called underground. Education still goes on, of course, but under a corrupt misdescription. A student studies a book, and this is reported on a form somewhere as an exercise in study 'skills'. A student comes to understand something, and his tutor writes down that the student's comprehension 'skills' have been enhanced. This sort of double-talk takes its toll. The more corrupt or supine teachers actually do become persuaded that their proper function is to offer training in transferable skills; and so they start to conspire with the official ideology in denying their students an education. This is a betrayal of the lives for which they are supposed to be helping to prepare.

Collingwood's philosophy of art shows with exemplary directness what sort of ethical and conceptual muddle lies at the heart of all this. The mistaking of purposeful activity for technical activity, the confounding of success with the successful realization of a preconceived end, the confusion of the hard task of clarification for the relatively easy one of classification: every element repeats the errors of the technical theory of art, and for just the same reasons. The substitution of so-called skills for education may not be fascism, exactly, or death. But it is certainly a form of corruption; and it is certainly worth inveighing against. It hasn't been inveighed against enough.

BIBLIOGRAPHY

Works Cited

Collingwood, R.G., *The Principles of Art* (Oxford University Press, Oxford, 1938). [Abbreviated in the text as *PA*]

Tolstoy, L., trans. Maude, A., *What is Art?* (Oxford University Press, Oxford, 1896).

Further Reading

Anderson, D.R., 'Artistic control in Collingwood's theory of art', *Journal of Aesthetics and Art Criticism*, 48:1 (1990): 53–9

Anderson, D.R. and Hausman, C.R., 'The role of emotion in R.G. Collingwood's conception of creative activity', *Journal of Aesthetics and Art Criticism*, 50:4 (1992): 299–305

Janaway, C., 'Arts and crafts in Plato and Collingwood', *Journal of Aesthetics and Art Criticism*, 50:1 (1992): 45–54

Johnson, P., *R.G. Collingwood: an Introduction* (Thoemmes Press, Bristol, 1998).

Jones, P., 'A critical outline of Collingwood's philosophy of art', in Krausz, M. (ed.), *Critical Essays on the Philosophy of R.G. Collingwood* (Oxford University Press, Oxford, 1972), pp.42–67

Ridley, A., 'Not ideal: Collingwood's expression theory', *Journal of Aesthetics and Art Criticism*, 55:3 (1997): 263–72

Wertz, S.K., 'The role of practice in Collingwood's theory of art', *Southwest Philosophical Review*, 11:1 (1995): 143–50

Wollheim, R., 'On an alleged inconsistency in Collingwood's aesthetic', in Krausz, M. (ed.), *Critical Essays on the Philosophy of R.G. Collingwood* (Oxford University Press, Oxford, 1972), pp.68–78

Wollheim, R., *Art and its Objects*, 2nd edn (Cambridge University Press, Cambridge, 1980), sections 22, 23, 45–52